PRETTY SIMPLE

~COLORING~

Love

45 Easy-to-Color Pages Inspired by Happiness and Love

T0066019

ADAMS MEDIA

NEW YORK   LONDON   TORONTO   SYDNEY   NEW DELHI

Adams Media
An Imprint of Simon & Schuster, Inc.
100 Technology Center Drive
Stoughton, Massachusetts 02072

Copyright © 2024 by Simon & Schuster, Inc.

All rights reserved, including the right to reproduce this book or portions thereof in any form whatsoever. For information, address Adams Media Subsidiary Rights Department, 1230 Avenue of the Americas, New York, NY 10020.

First Adams Media trade paperback edition January 2024

ADAMS MEDIA and colophon are registered trademarks of Simon & Schuster, Inc.

Simon & Schuster: Celebrating 100 Years of Publishing in 2024

For information about special discounts for bulk purchases, please contact Simon & Schuster Special Sales at 1-866-506-1949 or business@simonandschuster.com.

The Simon & Schuster Speakers Bureau can bring authors to your live event. For more information or to book an event, contact the Simon & Schuster Speakers Bureau at 1-866-248-3049 or visit our website at www.simonspeakers.com.

Interior images © 123RF; Getty Images

Manufactured in the United States of America

10 9 8 7 6 5 4 3 2 1

ISBN 978-1-5072-2158-7

Many of the designations used by manufacturers and sellers to distinguish their products are claimed as trademarks. Where those designations appear in this book and Simon & Schuster, Inc., was aware of a trademark claim, the designations have been printed with initial capital letters.

Introduction

Looking to do something creative, but don't have a lot of time?
Searching for an easy project to celebrate your feelings of love?
Or maybe you're trying to find a new way to relax?
The answer is pretty simple.

Take out your colored pencils, pens, crayons, or markers, and get ready to be creative and relieve your stress with the forty-five lovely, easy-to-color images in *Pretty Simple Coloring: Love*. Each page has a charming scene you can customize in the colors of your choosing. Unlike in other coloring books, these awesome images are designed with simple visual elements, which allow you to complete a page without a significant time commitment. And, because the art is easy to see with no complicated patterns, your eyes and hands will be less strained after your coloring sessions.

These easy, eye-catching designs also allow you to multitask if you want to. Color in beautiful hearts and sweet images while you listen to your favorite podcast, catch up on a new show, or follow the narration of your latest audiobook. However you choose to color, you can take a deep breath and let your stress melt away as you clear your mind and work on these pretty simple coloring pages.

Let your inner artist inspire your color palette. Feel free to use dreamy blues, greens, and purples if that's what makes your heart sing. Or maybe you feel more connected to a traditional Valentine's palette with reds and pinks. Let the pencils, pens, crayons, or markers inspire your hand, and personalize these gorgeous images as you see fit.

So whether your heart is overflowing with love, or you just want a stress-free way to color, it's time to dive into these simple, quick, and love-inspired pages, and get coloring.

Image © Getty Images/Anna Hlovatska

Image © 123RF/Nadezhda Aksenova

Image © Getty Images/Anna Hlovatska

Image © 123RF/Suryadi Djasman Kartodiwiryo

Image © Getty Images/Anna Hlovatska

Image © 123RF/catherinewhite

Image © Getty Images/Anna Hlovatska

Image © 123RF/Nadezhda Aksenova

Image © Getty Images/Anna Hlovatska

Image © 123RF/Nadezhda Aksenova

Image © Getty Images/Anna Hlovatska

Image © 123RF/maljuki

Image © Getty Images/Anna Hlovatska

Image © 123RF/catherinewhite

Image © Getty Images/Anna Hlovatska

Image © 123RF/nitoya chuahmon

Image © Getty Images/Aksenova Nadezhda

Image © 123RF/Svetlana Kutsin

Image © Getty Images/Aksenova Nadezhda

Image © 123RF/Valeria Holodnjak

Image © Getty Images/Oksana_Alekseeva

Image © 123RF/zagory

Image © 123RF/Nadezhda Aksenova

Image © 123RF/Nataliia Toporovska

Image © 123RF/Ohla Rakovets

Image © 123RF/Ellina Novokhatskaya

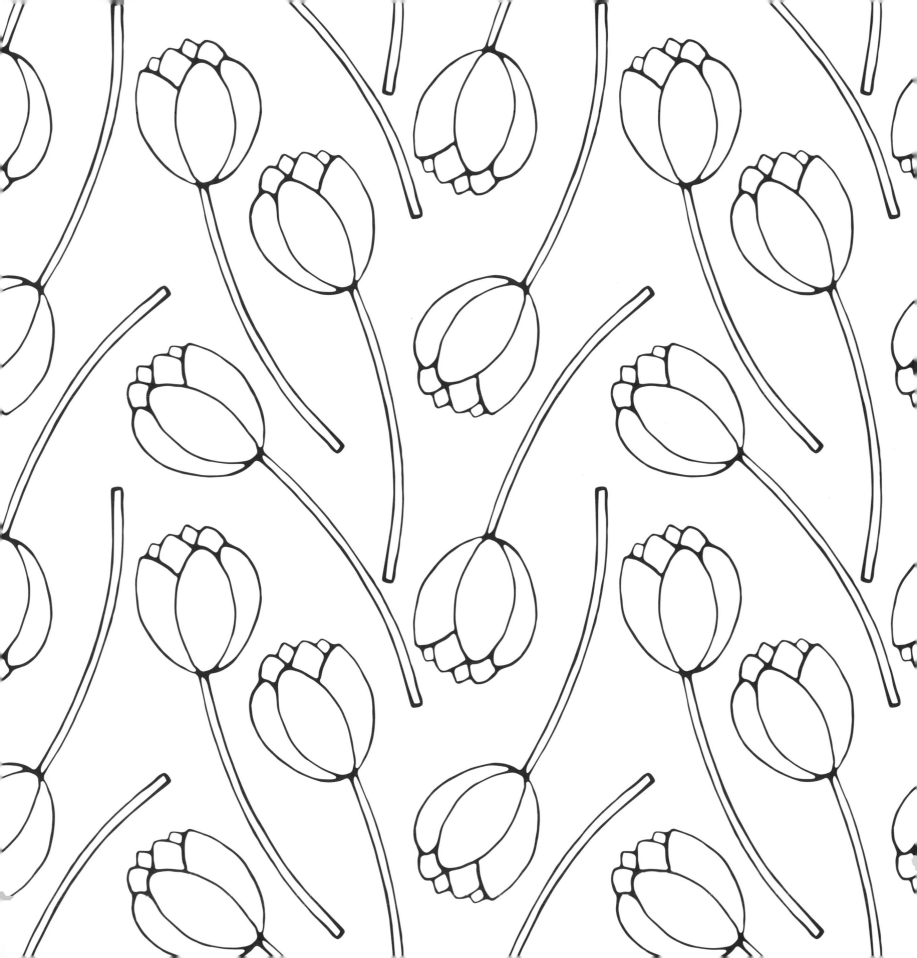

Image © 123RF/Iuliia Bessonova

Image © 123RF/Ohla Rakovets

Image © 123RF/Nadezhda Aksenova

Image © 123RF/sybirko

Image © 123RF/Nadezhda Aksenova

Image © 123RF/skywears

Image © 123RF/Elvira Shamilova

Image © Getty Images/natasha-tpr

Image © 123RF/zagory

Image © 123RF/Valeria Holodnjak

Image © 123RF/abadur rahman

Image © 123RF/Nadezhda Aksenova

Image © 123RF/Ekaterina Matveeva

Image © 123RF/kiyanochka

Image © 123RF/Nadezhda Aksenova

Image © 123RF/daniellabelaya

Image © 123RF/ipanki

Image © 123RF/maribryk

Image © 123RF/verock42

MAKE THE MOST OF YOUR FREE TIME!

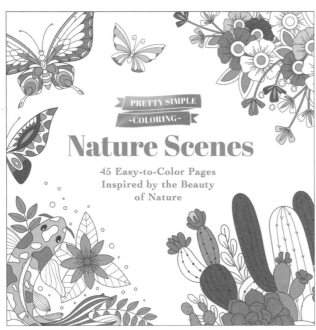

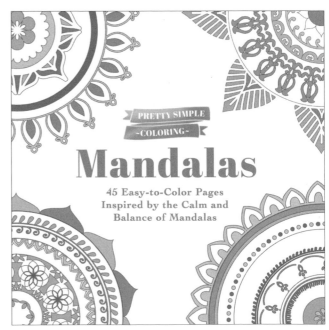

Pick Up Your Copies Today!

adamsmedia
An Imprint of Simon & Schuster
A Paramount Company